PIANO/VOCAL/GUITAR

GOD BLESS AMERICA®

ABOUT "GOD BLESS AMERICA"

"GOD BLESS AMERICA" by Irving Berlin was first published in 1938. Almost as soon as the song began generating revenue, Mr. Berlin established The God Bless America Fund to benefit American youth.

Over $6,000,000 has been distributed to date, primarily to two youth organizations with which Mr. and Mrs. Berlin were personally involved: the Girl Scout Council of Greater New York, and the Greater New York Councils of the Boy Scouts of America. These councils do not discriminate on any basis and are committed to serving all segments of New York City's diverse youth population.

The trustees of The God Bless America Fund are working with the two councils to ensure that funding is allocated for New York City children affected by the tragic events of September 11, 2001.

GOD BLESS AMERICA is a registered trademark of the Trustees of The God Bless America Fund.

ISBN 0-634-04121-5

HAL•LEONARD®
CORPORATION

7777 W. BLUEMOUND RD. P.O. BOX 13819 MILWAUKEE, WI 53213

Visit Hal Leonard Online at
www.halleonard.com

GOD BLESS AMERICA

Words and Music by
IRVING BERLIN

LAND OF HOPE AND DREAMS

Words and Music by
BRUCE SPRINGSTEEN

train; hear the steel wheels sing-in'. This __ train; bells of free-dom ring. __

Instrumental solo

Solo ends

Well, __ this

HERO

Words and Music by MARIAH CAREY
and WALTER AFANASIEFF

AMAZING GRACE

Words, Music and Arrangement by TRAMAINE HAWKINS
and MARTY PAICH

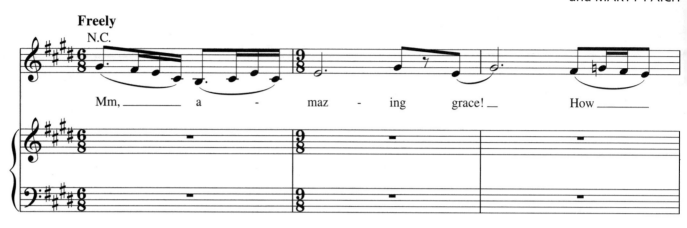

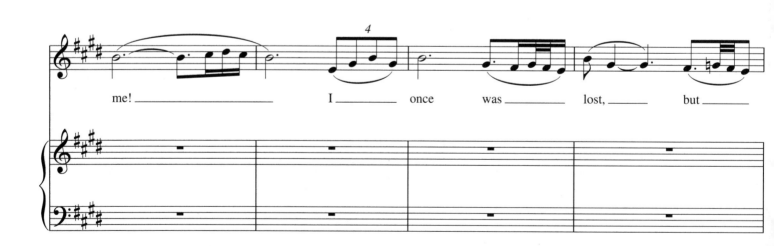

saved a _____ wretch like _ me! _____ I _____

once _____ was _____ lost, _____ but now, _____ right now, _ I'm

found; _____ I _____ was blind, _ but _____ now I

see. _____

BLOWIN' IN THE WIND

Words and Music by
BOB DYLAN

Yes,   and

BRIDGE OVER TROUBLED WATER

Words and Music by
PAUL SIMON

I'm sail- ing right be - hind. ___ Like a bridge o - ver

trou- bled wa- ter, I will ease your mind. ___ Like a bridge o - ver

trou- bled wa- ter, I will ease your mind. _____

rall.

PEACEFUL WORLD

Words and Music by
JOHN MELLENCAMP

THERE'S A HERO

Words and Music by DON COOK
and JOHN JARVIS

ev - 'ry - bod - y's heart. _____

Go on and trust your - self; _____ you can

AMERICA THE BEAUTIFUL

Words by KATHERINE LEE BATES
Music by SAMUEL AUGUSTUS WARD

GOD BLESS THE U.S.A.

Words and Music by
LEE GREENWOOD

If to-mor-row all the things were gone I'd worked for all my life and I had to start a-gain with just my chil-dren and my wife, I'd thank my luck-y stars to be

Am7

Gm7

liv - in' here __ to - day, __ 'cause the flag still stands for free - dom and they

Dm

B♭

can't take that a - way. _____ And I'm

C/E

B♭/D

F

proud to be an A - mer - i - can __ where at least I know I'm free. And I

C/E

B♭/D

F

won't for - get the men who died, who gave that right to me. And I'd glad - ly

THIS LAND IS YOUR LAND

Words and Music by
WOODY GUTHRIE

Bright and cheerfully

As I went

(1.) walk - ing ____ that rib - bon of high - way ____ I saw a -
(2.,4.,6.) your land, ____ this land is my land, ____ from Cal - i -
(3.) ram - bled ____ and I fol - lowed my foot - steps ____ to the spar - kling
(5.) shin - ing, ____ and I was stroll - ing; ____ the wheat fields

bove me ____ that end - less sky - way; ____ I saw be -
for - nia ____ to the New York is - land; ____ from the red - wood
sands ____ of her dia - mond des - erts; ____ while all a -
wav - ing ____ and the dust clouds roll - ing. ____ The fog was

COMING OUT OF THE DARK

Words and Music by GLORIA ESTEFAN
EMILIO ESTEFAN, JR. and JON SECADA

WE SHALL OVERCOME

Musical and Lyrical Adaptation by ZILPHIA HORTON,
FRANK HAMILTON, GUY CARAWAN and PETE SEEGER
Inspired by African American Gospel Singing,
members of the Food and Tobacco Workers Union, Charleston, SC,
and the southern Civil Rights Movement

THE STAR SPANGLED BANNER

Words by FRANCIS SCOTT KEY
Music by JOHN STAFFORD SMITH
Arranged by FRANK W. ASPER

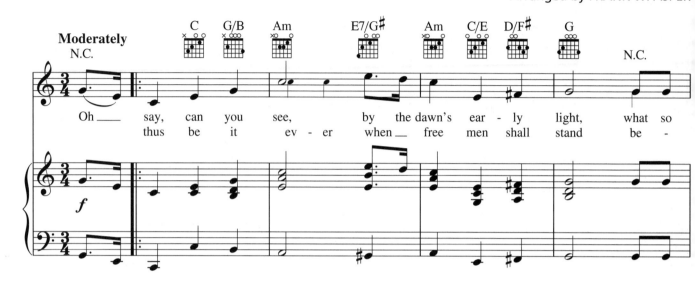

Oh ___ say, can you see, by the dawn's ear-ly light, what so
thus be it ev-er when ___ free men shall stand what be-

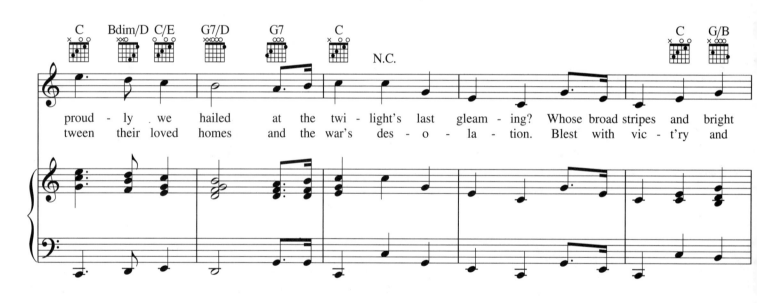

proud-ly we hailed at the twi-light's last gleam-ing? Whose broad stripes and bright
tween their loved homes and the war's des-o-la-tion. Blest with vic-t'ry and

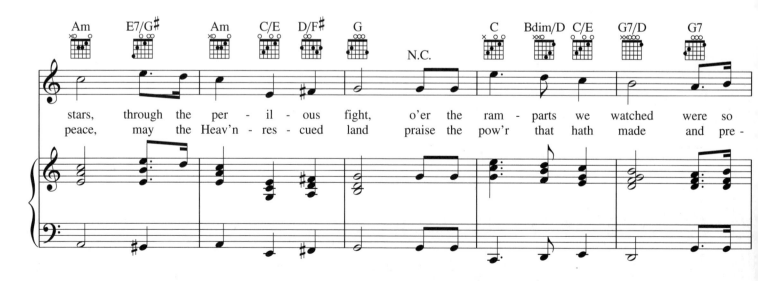

stars, through the per-il-ous fight, o'er the ram-parts we watched were so
peace, may the Heav'n-res-cued land praise the pow'r that hath made and pre-

LEAN ON ME

Words and Music by
BILL WITHERS

C Dm Em F Em Dm C
for it won't be long 'til I'm gon - na need
C/E F C/F♯ G7 C
some - bod - y to lean on.
Dm Em F Em Dm C
Please swal - low your pride if I have things
C/E F6 G6 C/G G9
you need to bor - row,
8vb